Sight Reading
VIOLA
A progressive method
Initial-Grade 2

Celia Cobb &
Naomi Yandell

Published by
Trinity College London Press Ltd
trinitycollege.com

Registered in England
Company no. 09726123

Copyright © 2020 Trinity College London Press Ltd
Second impression, January 2021

Unauthorised photocopying is illegal
No part of this publication may be copied or reproduced in any
form or by any means without the prior permission of the publisher.

Cover design by RF Design, rfportfolio.com
Printed in England by Halstan & Co, Amersham, Bucks

Initial

Lesson 1

- Practise feeling a steady pulse
- Practise reading the note values crotchet and minim

♩ **crotchet.** A crotchet lasts for one beat.

𝅗𝅥 **minim.** A minim lasts for two beats.

Tap each exercise on the back of your viola.

1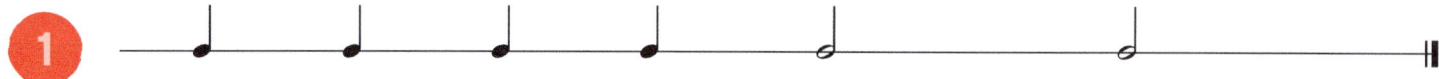

2

3

4

5

Initial

Think before you tap:

Is your rhythm the same as your teacher's?   Yes ☐   No ☐

How long does each minim last?   One crotchet beat ☐   Two crotchet beats ☐

Circle all the minims in your part.

(This section applies to the duet below.)

Duet — Your teacher will count two crotchet beats to show the pulse before you play.

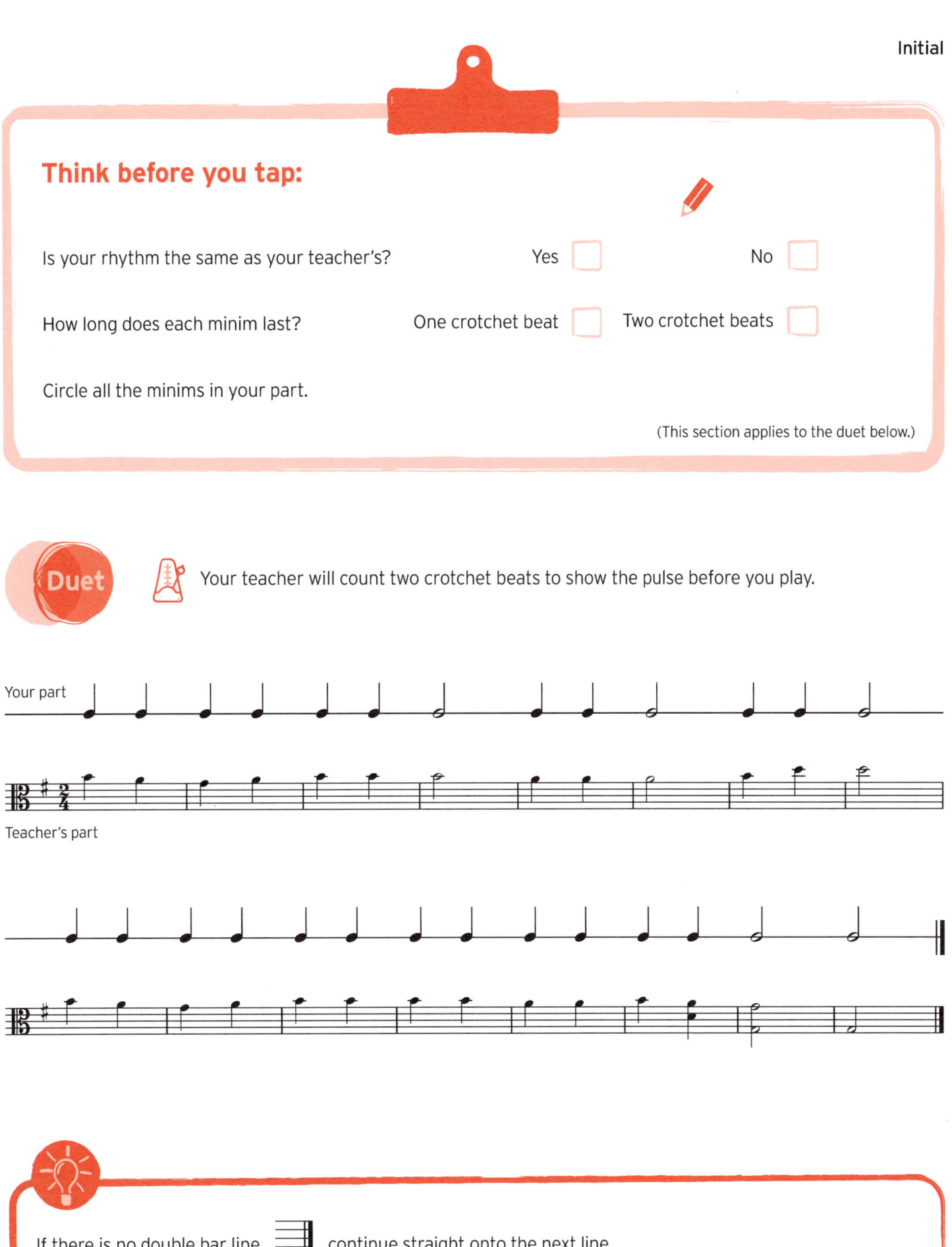

If there is no double bar line 𝄁 continue straight onto the next line.

Initial

Lesson 2

- **Practise reading in the time signatures 2/4 and 4/4**

  2/4 two crotchet beats in a bar.

  4/4 four crotchet beats in a bar.

Tap each exercise on the back of your viola.

1)
2)
3)
4)
5)

Initial

Think before you tap:

How many crotchet beats are there in each bar?   Two ☐   Four ☐

Is your rhythm the same as your teacher's?   Yes ☐   No ☐

Circle the bar in which your part has only minims.

   Your teacher will count four crotchet beats to show the pulse before you play.

Bar lines ┤ divide the music into bars. The time signature tells you how many beats will be in each bar.

Initial

Lesson 3

- Practise reading the note G as a crotchet or a minim

G
(crotchet)

G
(minim)

Play each exercise on your viola.

1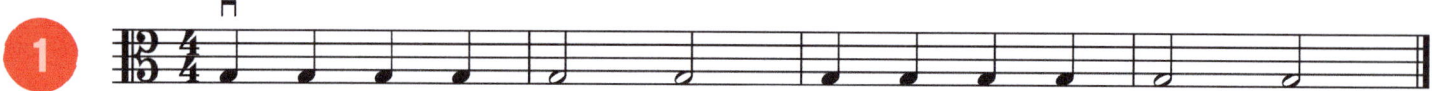

2

3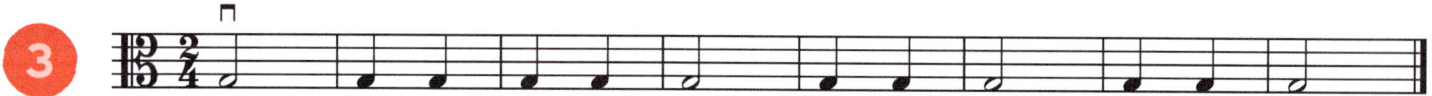

4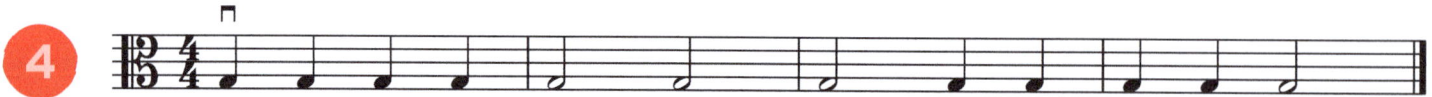

5

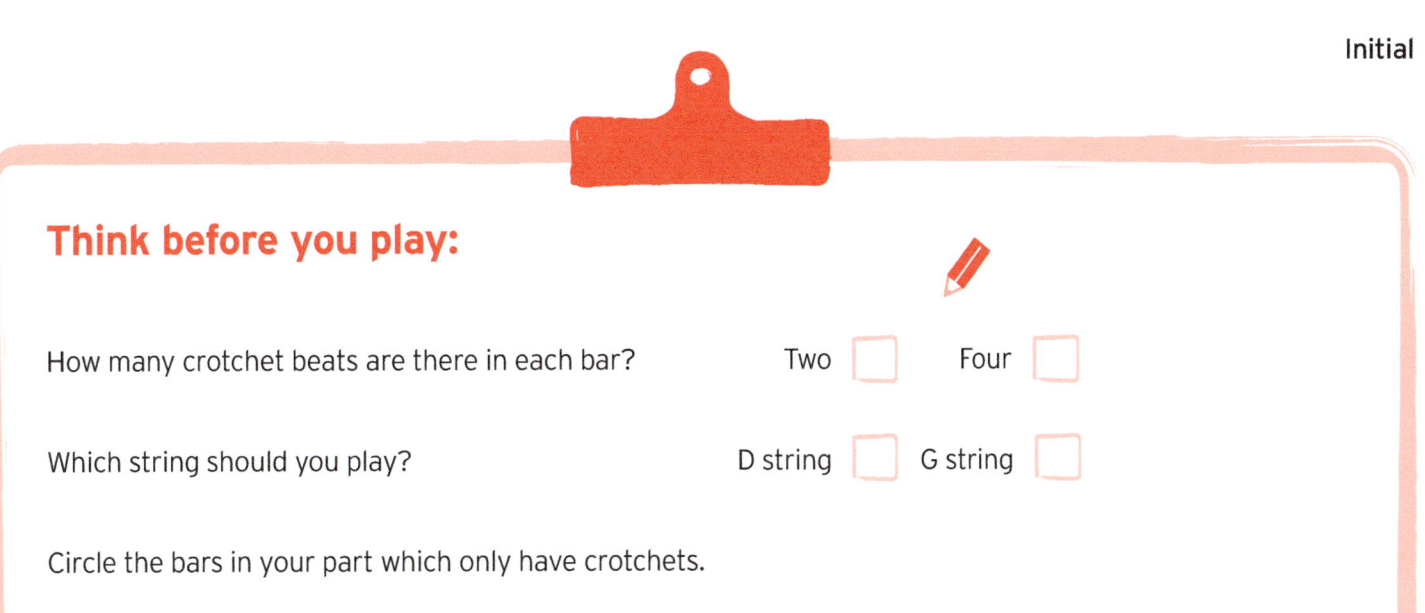

Think before you play:

How many crotchet beats are there in each bar?   Two ☐   Four ☐

Which string should you play?   D string ☐   G string ☐

Circle the bars in your part which only have crotchets.

 Your teacher will count four crotchet beats to show the pulse before you play.

⊓ means down bow.

Initial

Lesson 4

- Practise reading the note D as a crotchet or a minim

D
(crotchet)

D
(minim)

Play each exercise on your viola.

1

2

3

4
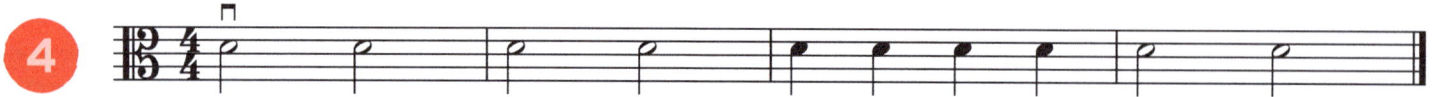

5

Initial

Think before you play:

How many crotchet beats are there in each bar?   Two ☐   Four ☐

Which string should you play?   D string ☐   G string ☐

Which exercise on page 8 has the same rhythm as line 1 of your part?   2 ☐   3 ☐

 Your teacher will count two crotchet beats to show the pulse before you play.

 Feel the pulse as you play.

Initial

Lesson 5

- Practise reading the note C as a crotchet or a minim
- Learn to spot rhythm-patterns

C (crotchet)   C (minim)

Circle the repeating rhythm-patterns then play each exercise on your viola.

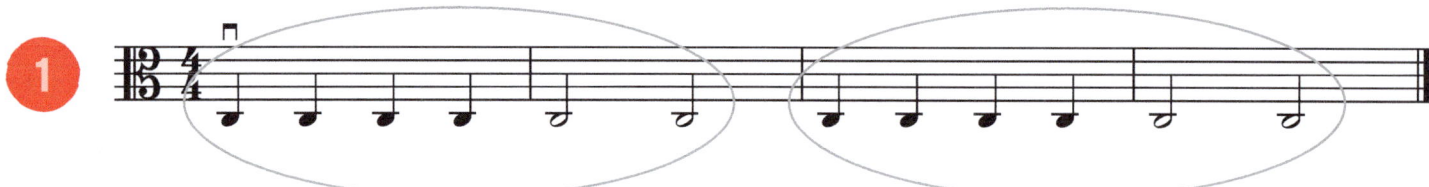

Initial

Think before you play:

Which string should you play? D string ☐ C string ☐

In how many bars do you only play crotchets? Two ☐ Four ☐

Circle the bars in your part which have the rhythm-pattern ♩ ♩ ♩

 Set the pulse: count four crotchet beats before you play.

Keep going! If you make a mistake, just play on.

Initial

Lesson 6

- Practise reading the note A as a crotchet or a minim

A
(crotchet)

A
(minim)

Circle the repeating rhythm-patterns then play each exercise on your viola.

1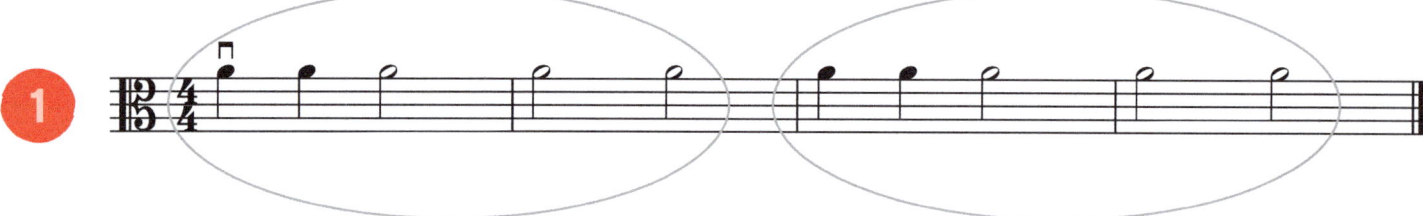

2

3

4

5

Initial

Think before you play:

Which string should you play?   A string ☐   G string ☐

How many minims are there in your part?   Three ☐   Four ☐

Circle the bars in which your rhythm is different to your teacher's.

 Set the pulse: count two crotchet beats before you play.

When your rhythm is different to your teacher's, keep the pulse going in your head and play on.

Initial

Lesson 7

- **Practise reading exercises on two strings: G and D**
- **Revise the meaning of *mf***

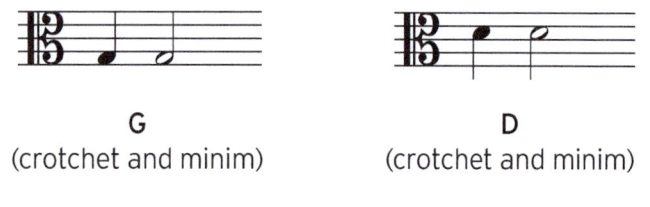

G
(crotchet and minim)

D
(crotchet and minim)

mf means play moderately loudly.

Circle the notes that will sound highest, then play each exercise on your viola.

1.

2.

3.

4.

5.

Initial

Think before you play:

Which string should you play first? D string ☐ G string ☐

Circle the bars in which your rhythm is different to your teacher's.

In your part, how many times do you see the rhythm-pattern ♩ ♩ ♩ ? Two ☐ Three ☐

 Duet   Set the pulse: count two crotchet beats before you play.

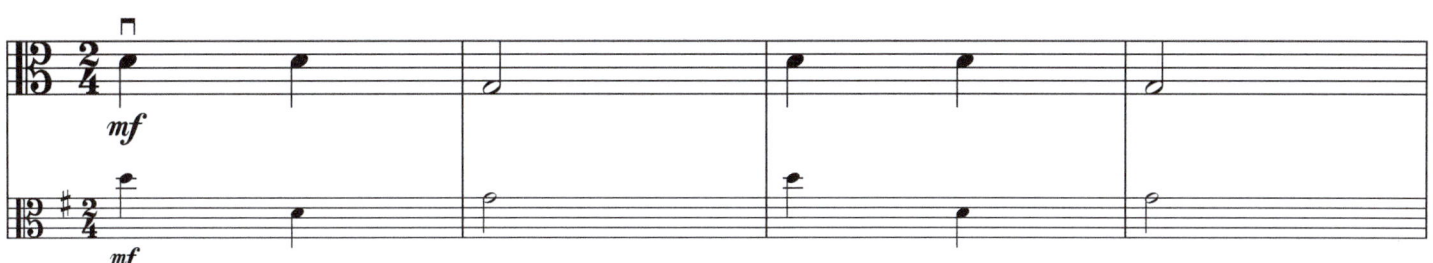

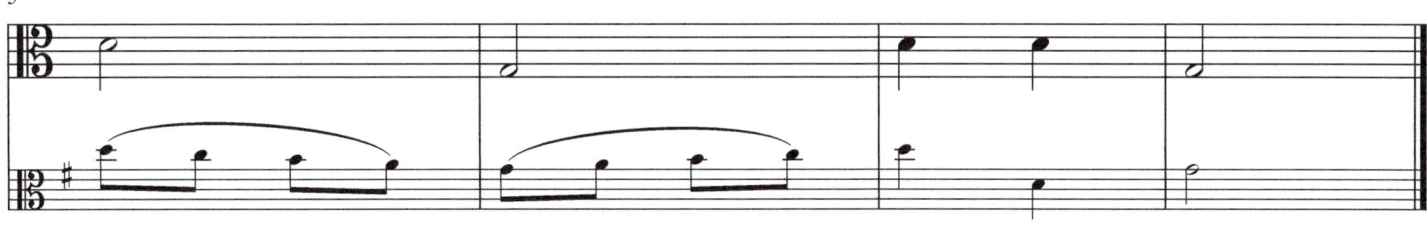

 Notes that look higher will also sound higher.

Initial

Lesson 8

- Practise reading exercises on two strings: C and G
- Revise the meaning of *Moderato*

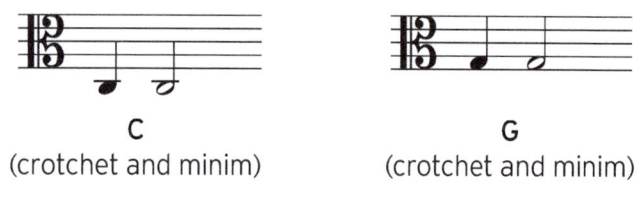

C
(crotchet and minim)

G
(crotchet and minim)

Moderato means play at a moderate tempo.

Circle the notes that will sound lowest, then play each exercise on your viola.

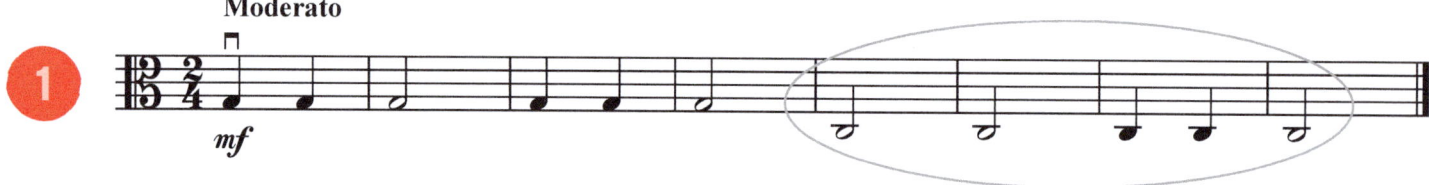

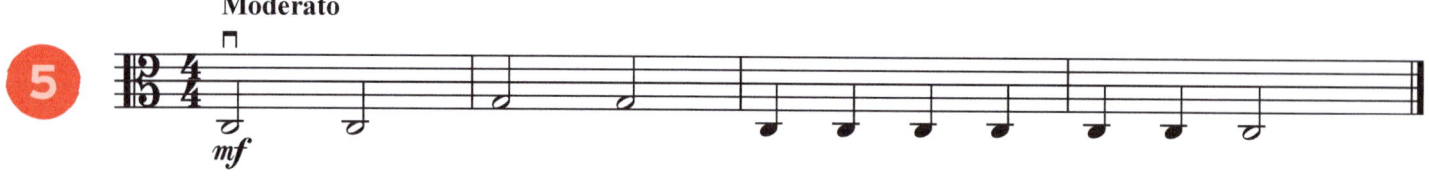

Initial

Think before you play:

Which string should you play first?   C string ☐   G string ☐

Circle the bar(s) in which your rhythm is different to your teacher's.

Compare bars 1-3 and bars 5-7 in your part.   They are different ☐   They are the same ☐

 Set the pulse: count a whole bar of crotchets before you play.

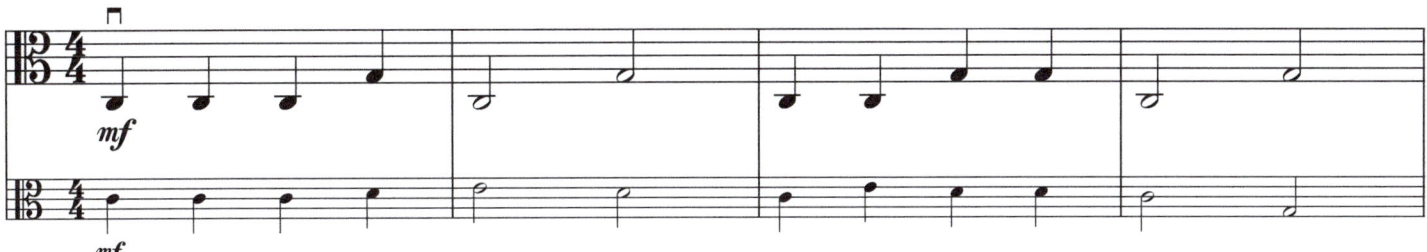

Notes that should sound together in a duet appear above one another, like this:

Initial

Lesson 9

- Practise reading exercises on two strings: D and A
- Learn to spot rhythm and tune patterns

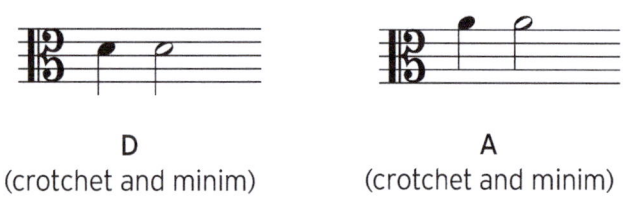

D
(crotchet and minim)

A
(crotchet and minim)

Circle the repeating patterns, then play each exercise on your viola.

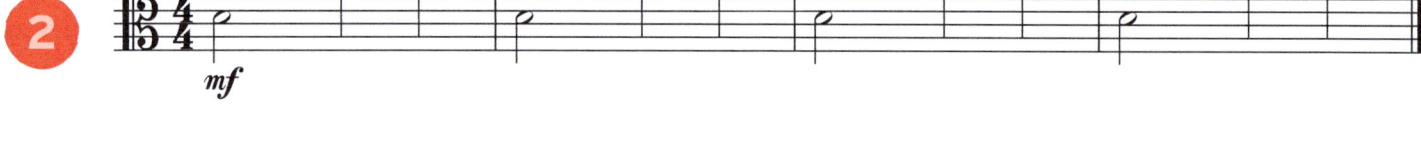

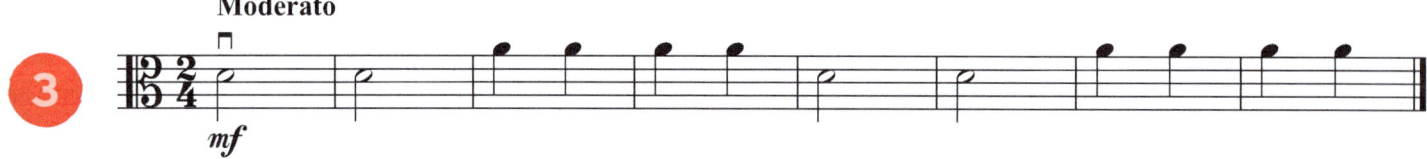

Initial

Think before you play:

Which string should you play first?   A string ☐   D string ☐

Compare bars 1-4 and bars 5-8 in your part.   They are different ☐   They are the same ☐

Circle the bars in which your rhythm is the same as your teacher's.

 Set the pulse: count a whole bar of crotchets before you play.

Think about the way you use your bow. You will usually need to use more bow for longer notes.

Initial

Lesson 10

- Practise reading exercises on three strings: (G, D and A) or (C, G and D)

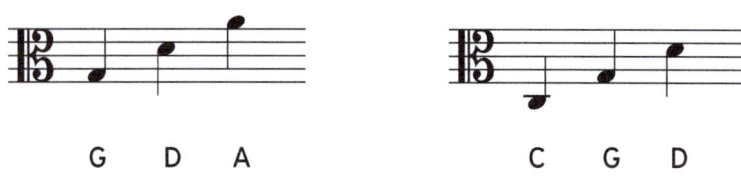

G D A   C G D

Tick the exercises which use G, D and A. Then play each exercise on your viola.

1

2

3

4

5

Initial

Think before you play:

Which strings should you play?   G, D and A ☐   C, G and D ☐

How many bars in your part have the rhythm-pattern 𝅗𝅥 ♩ ♩ ?   Seven ☐   Eight ☐

In which bars should you play the same rhythm as your teacher?   Every bar ☐   Bars 4 and 8 ☐

Duet — Set the pulse: count a whole bar of crotchets before you play.

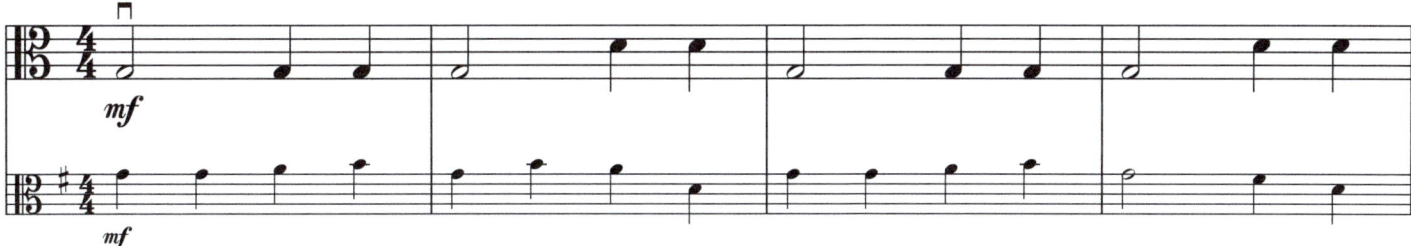

Always look out for repeating patterns.

Initial

Specimen sight reading tests

Remember to use the ideas and techniques from the previous lessons when sight reading these tests.

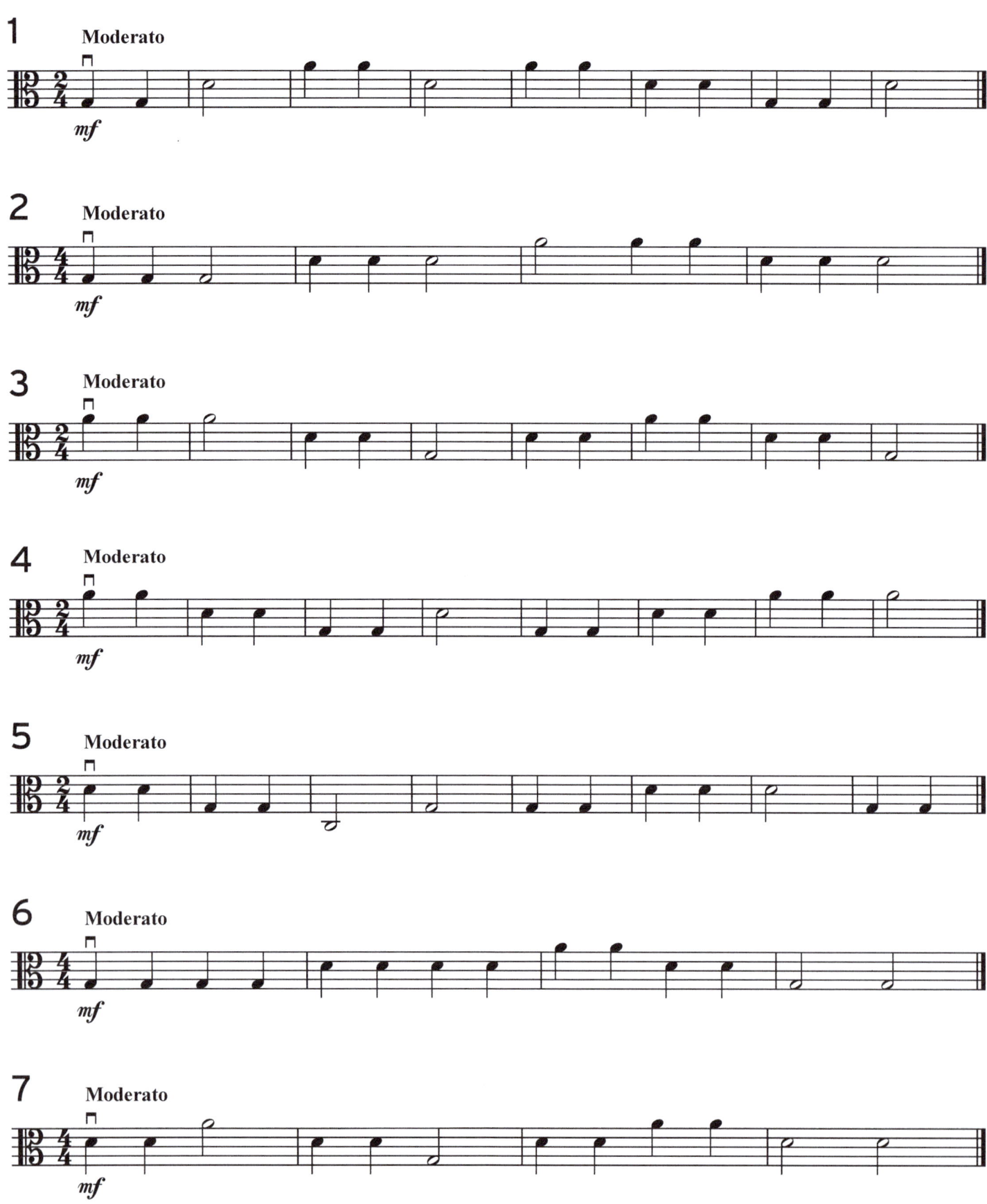

Grade 1

Lesson 1

- **Practise reading the notes A, B, C♯ and D on the A string, moving by step or staying the same**
- **Revise the meaning of _f_**

In the key of D major, the notes on the A string are A, B, C♯ and D.

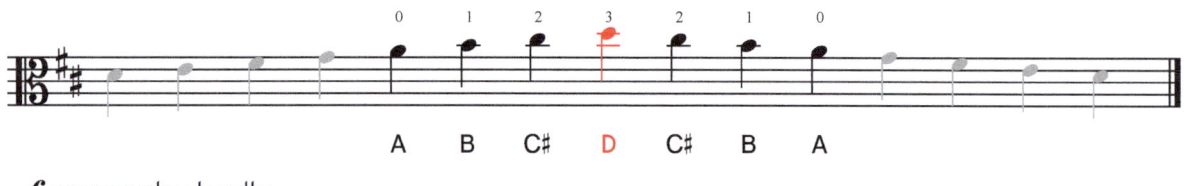

A   B   C♯   D   C♯   B   A

_f_ means play loudly.

Play each exercise first as a rhythm on your open A string. Then play the whole exercise as written.

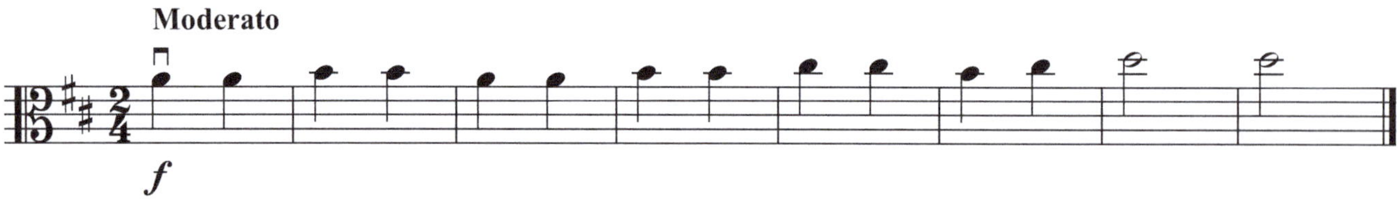

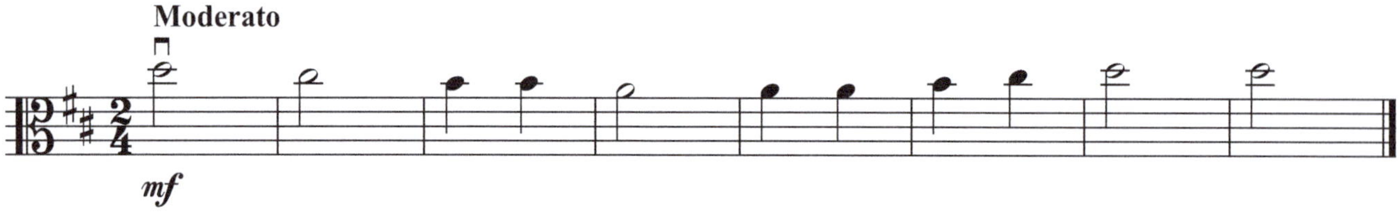

Grade 1

Think before you play:

Name the first note in your part.　　　　　　　　　　　　　　A ☐　　B ☐

Look at bars 5 and 6 in your part. Are they different or the same?　Different ☐　The same ☐

At what dynamic should you play this piece?　　　Moderately loud ☐　Loud ☐

Duet　　Set the pulse: count a whole bar of crotchets before you play.

Setting the pulse before you start helps you to keep the beat in your head all the way through the piece.

25

Grade 1

Lesson 2

- **Practise reading the notes D, E, F♯ and G on the D string, moving by step or staying the same**

In D major, the notes on the D string are D, E, F♯ and G.

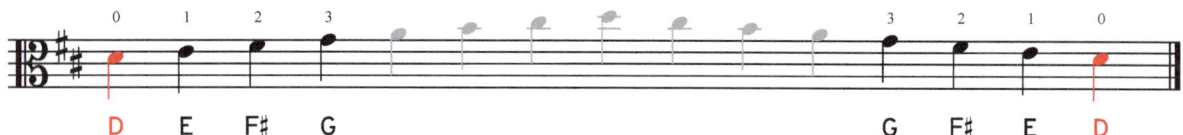

In G major, the notes on the D string are also D, E, F♯ and G.

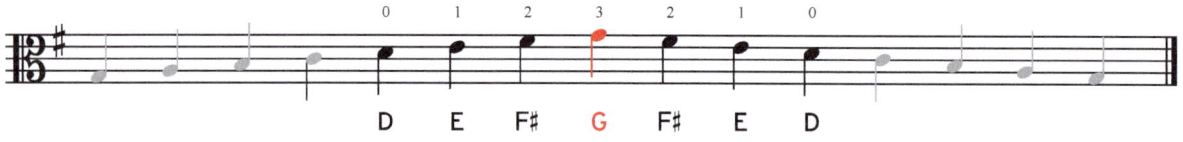

Play each exercise first as a rhythm on your open D string. Then play the whole exercise as written.

1

2

3

4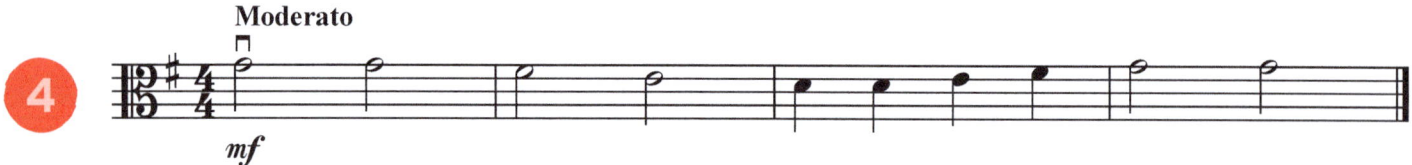

5

26

Grade 1

Think before you play:

How many crotchet beats are there in each bar?		Two ☐		Four ☐
On which string should you play?		D string ☐		G string ☐
Which exercise on page 26 has the same rhythm as line 1 of your part?		3 ☐		4 ☐

 Set the pulse: count a whole bar of crotchets before you play.

Speed read your part before you play so that you know what is coming up.

Grade 1

Lesson 3

- Practise reading the notes G, A, B and C on the G string, moving by step or staying the same

In G major, the notes on the G string are G, A, B and C.

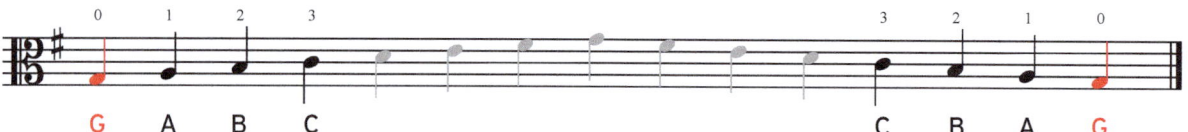

In C major, the notes on the G string are also G, A, B and C.

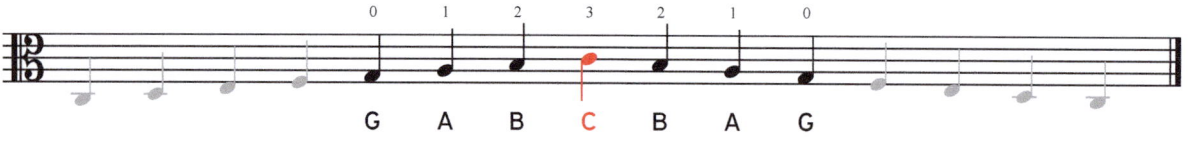

Play each exercise first as a rhythm on your open G string. Then play the whole exercise as written.

1

2

3

4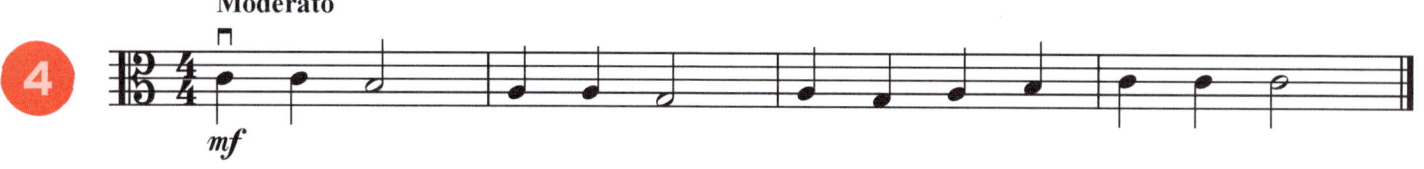

5

Grade 1

Think before you play:

On which string should you play? G string ☐ D string ☐

How many bars in your part have the rhythm-pattern ♩ ♩ ♩ ? Two ☐ Three ☐

In which bars do the notes stay at the same pitch? Bars 1, 5 & 8 ☐ Bars 1, 3 & 7 ☐

Set the pulse: count a whole bar of crotchets before you play.

Prepare your left-hand fingers before you play, so that you begin on the correct note.

Grade 1

Lesson 4

- Practise reading the notes C, D, E and F on the C string, moving by step or staying the same

In C major, the notes on the C string are C, D, E and F.

Play each exercise first as a rhythm on your open C string. Then play the whole exercise as written.

1

2

3

4

5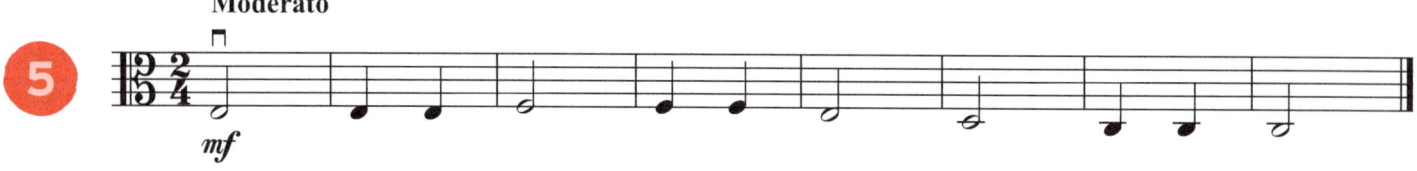

Grade 1

Think before you play:

How many crotchet beats are there in each bar?   Two ☐   Four ☐

Is your rhythm the same as the teacher's part throughout?   Yes ☐   No ☐

Which finger should you use to play the first note?   0 ☐   3 ☐

 Set the pulse: count a whole bar of crotchets before you play.

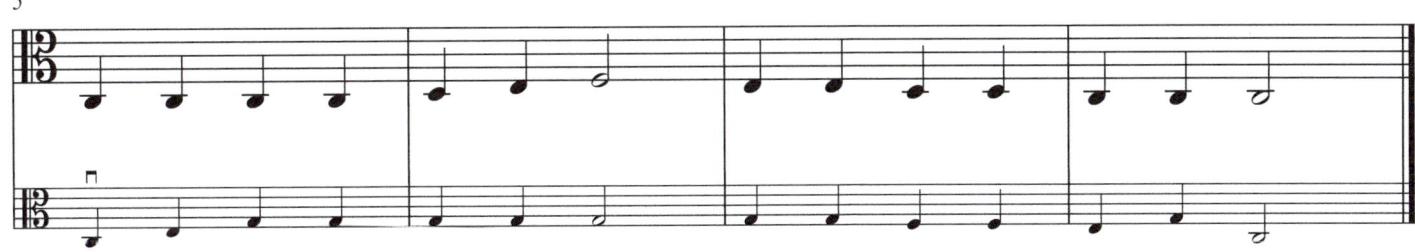

Follow the shape of the notes: if they go up, play up the scale. If they go down, play down the scale. If they stay the same, play the same note.

Grade 1

Lesson 5

- Practise reading the notes C, D, E and F on the C string, moving by step, by intervals of a 3rd or 4th or staying the same

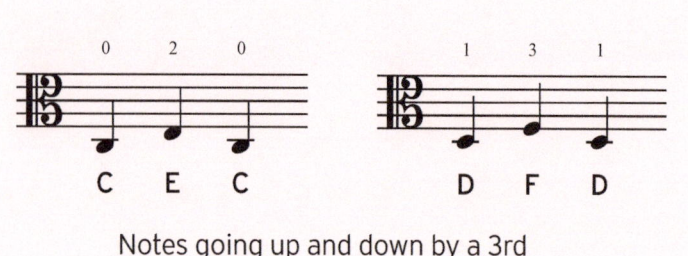

Notes going up and down by a 3rd

Notes going up and down by a 4th

Circle the 3rds, then play each exercise as a rhythm on your open C string.
Finally play the whole exercise as written.

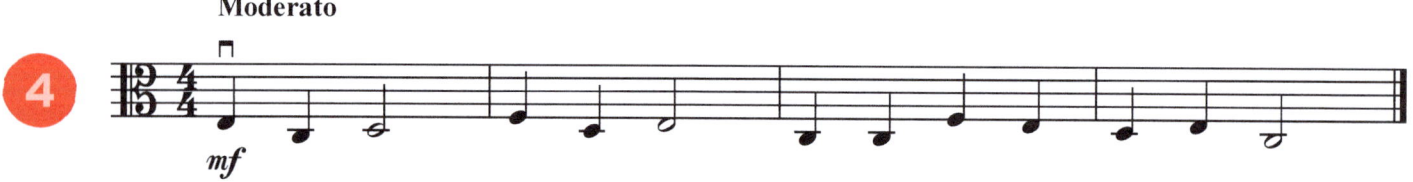

Grade 1

Think before you play:

Name the first note in your part. C ☐   E ☐

Where in your part do bars 1-2 repeat?   Bars 7-8 ☐   Bars 5-6 ☐

How loudly should you play?   Moderately loud ☐   Loud ☐

 Set the pulse: think four crotchets and breathe in on the last one before you play.

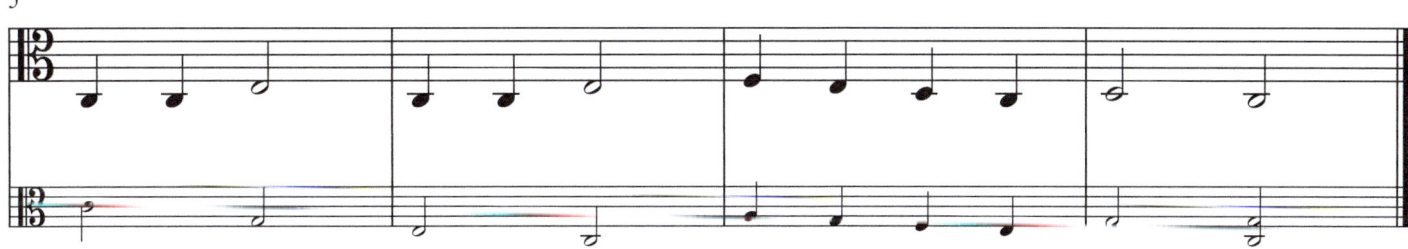

It is always useful to play unfamiliar music as a rhythm on the appropriate open string(s), before you add in the left-hand fingers. However, this isn't always possible when you sight read.

Grade 1

Lesson 6

- Practise reading the notes G, A, B and C on the G string, moving by step, by intervals of a 3rd or 4th, or staying the same

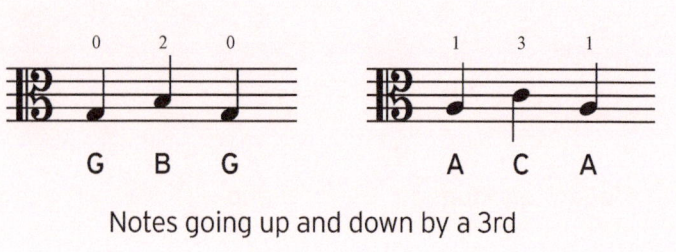

Notes going up and down by a 3rd

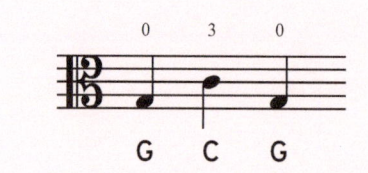

Notes going up and down by a 4th

Circle the 4ths, then play each exercise as a rhythm on your open G string.
Finally play the whole exercise as written.

1

2

3

4

5

Grade 1

Think before you play:

On which string should you play? C string ☐   G string ☐

How many intervals of a 3rd are there in your part? One ☐   Two ☐

In which bar should you only play Gs? Bar 3 ☐   Bar 7 ☐

Duet Set the pulse: think four crotchets and breathe in on the last one before you play.

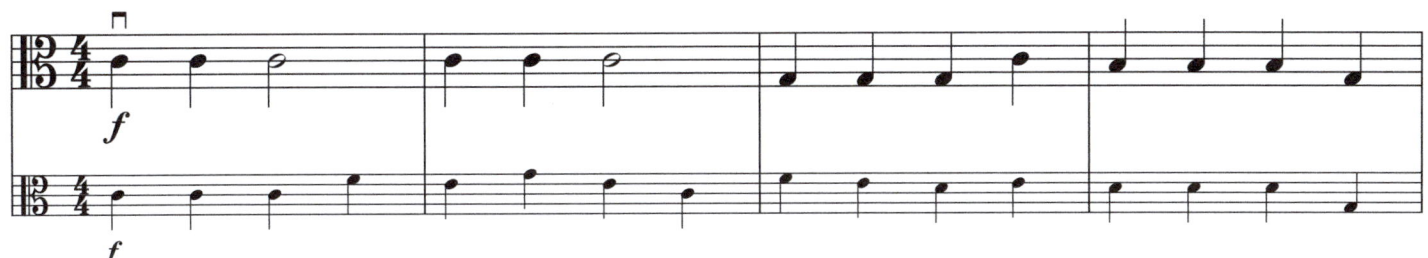

In G major, the notes on the G string are G, A, B and C.

In C major, the notes on the G string are also G, A, B and C.

35

Grade 1

Lesson 7

- Practise reading the notes D, E, F♯ and G on the D string, moving by step, by intervals of a 3rd or 4th, or staying the same

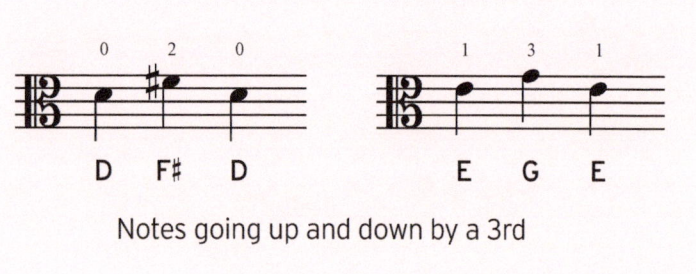

Notes going up and down by a 3rd

Notes going up and down by a 4th

Circle the 3rds, then play each exercise as a rhythm on your open D string.
Finally play the whole exercise as written.

1

2

3

4

5

Grade 1

Think before you play:

Which finger should you use to play the first note?   2 ☐   3 ☐

How many times should you play the rhythm-pattern ?   Four ☐   Six ☐

Bars 1–4 are louder than bars 5–8.   True ☐   False ☐

 Set the pulse: think four crotchets and breathe in on the last one before you play.

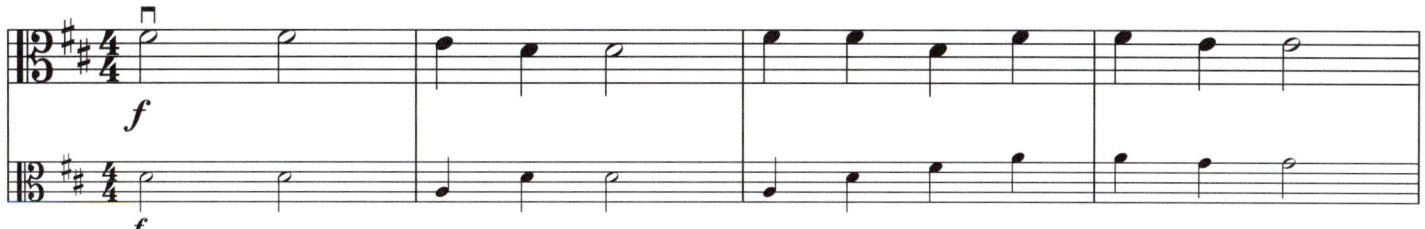

 In D major, the notes on the D string are D, E, F♯ and G.

 In G major, the notes on the D string are also D, E, F♯ and G.

37

Grade 1

Lesson 8

- Practise reading the notes A, B, C♯ and D on the A string, moving by step, by intervals of a 3rd or 4th or staying the same
- Revise the meaning of *p*

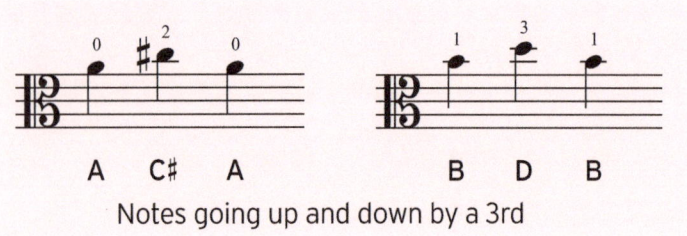
Notes going up and down by a 3rd

Notes going up and down by a 4th

p means play softly.

Play each exercise first as a rhythm on your open A string. Then play the whole exercise as written.

1
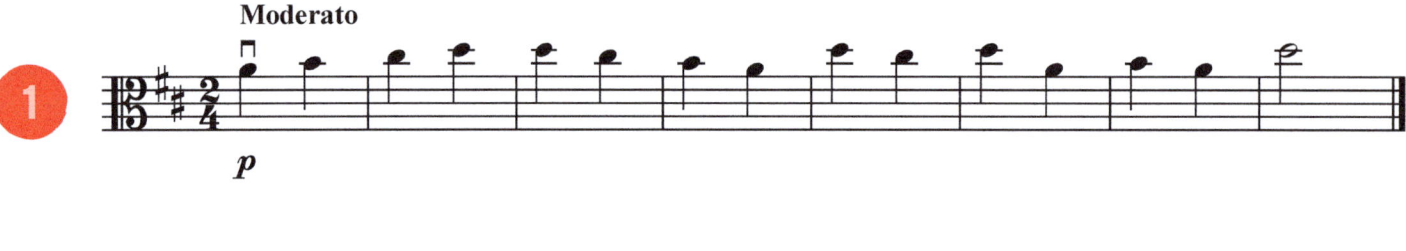

2
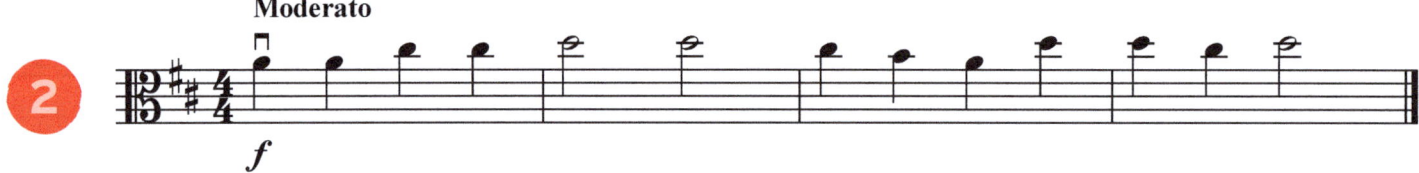

3
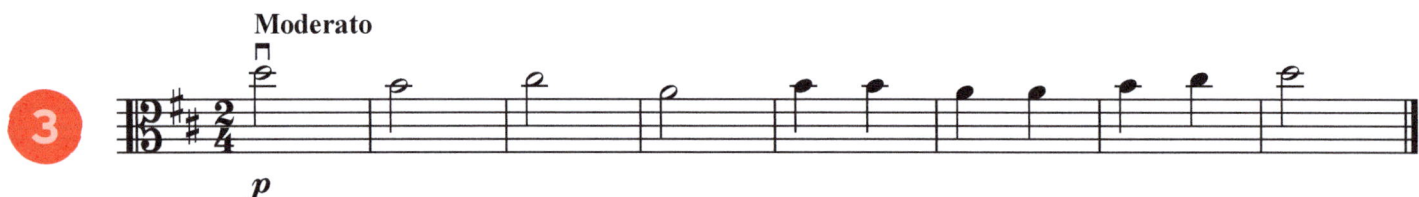

4
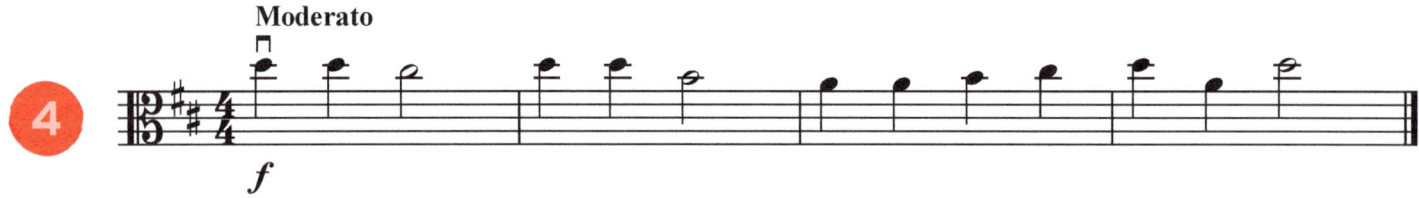

5

Grade 1

Think before you play:

On which string should you play?   A string ☐   D string ☐

Which finger should you use to play the first note?   1 ☐   3 ☐

Circle the bars where your rhythm is different from your teacher's.

 Set the pulse: think four crotchets and breathe in on the last one before you play.

 Look ahead. While you play open strings prepare your hand for the next fingered note.
Remember, if you have time, it is a good idea to play unfamiliar music on open strings first.

39

Grade 1

Lesson 9

- Practise reading five-note patterns starting on the C or G string
- Recognise where to change strings

Playing each exercise on open strings before adding the fingers will really help to spot the string changes.

Play each exercise first as a rhythm on the appropriate open strings. Then circle the string changes and play the whole exercise as written.

Grade 1

Think before you play:

At which dynamic should you play?   Loud ☐   Soft ☐

How many times will you have to change string in bars 5 and 6?   Three ☐   Five ☐

In which bars should you change string?   Bars 1, 2 & 3 ☐   Bars 5, 6 & 7 ☐

 Set the pulse: think four crotchets and breathe in on the last one before you play.

 Keep a look out for rhythm and tune patterns and remember to play through on open strings first if you have time.

Grade 1

Lesson 10

- Practise reading five-note patterns starting on the G or D string
- Recognise where to change strings

Playing each exercise on open strings before adding the fingers will really help to spot the string changes.

Play each exercise first as a rhythm on the appropriate open strings. Then circle the string changes and play the whole exercise as written.

1

2

3

4

5

Grade 1

Think before you play:

Which strings should you play? D and A ☐   G and D ☐

Draw a circle around the first note where you should change string.

In your part, the rhythm in bars 2 and 4 is: The same ☐   Different ☐

 Set the pulse: think four crotchets and breathe in on the last one before you play.

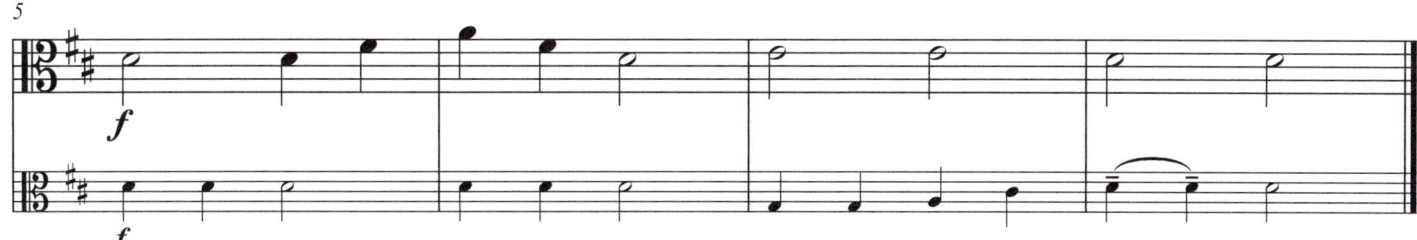

Good sight readers notice details, such as changes in dynamics.

Grade 1

Specimen sight reading tests

Remember to use the ideas and techniques from the previous lessons when sight reading these tests.

Grade 1

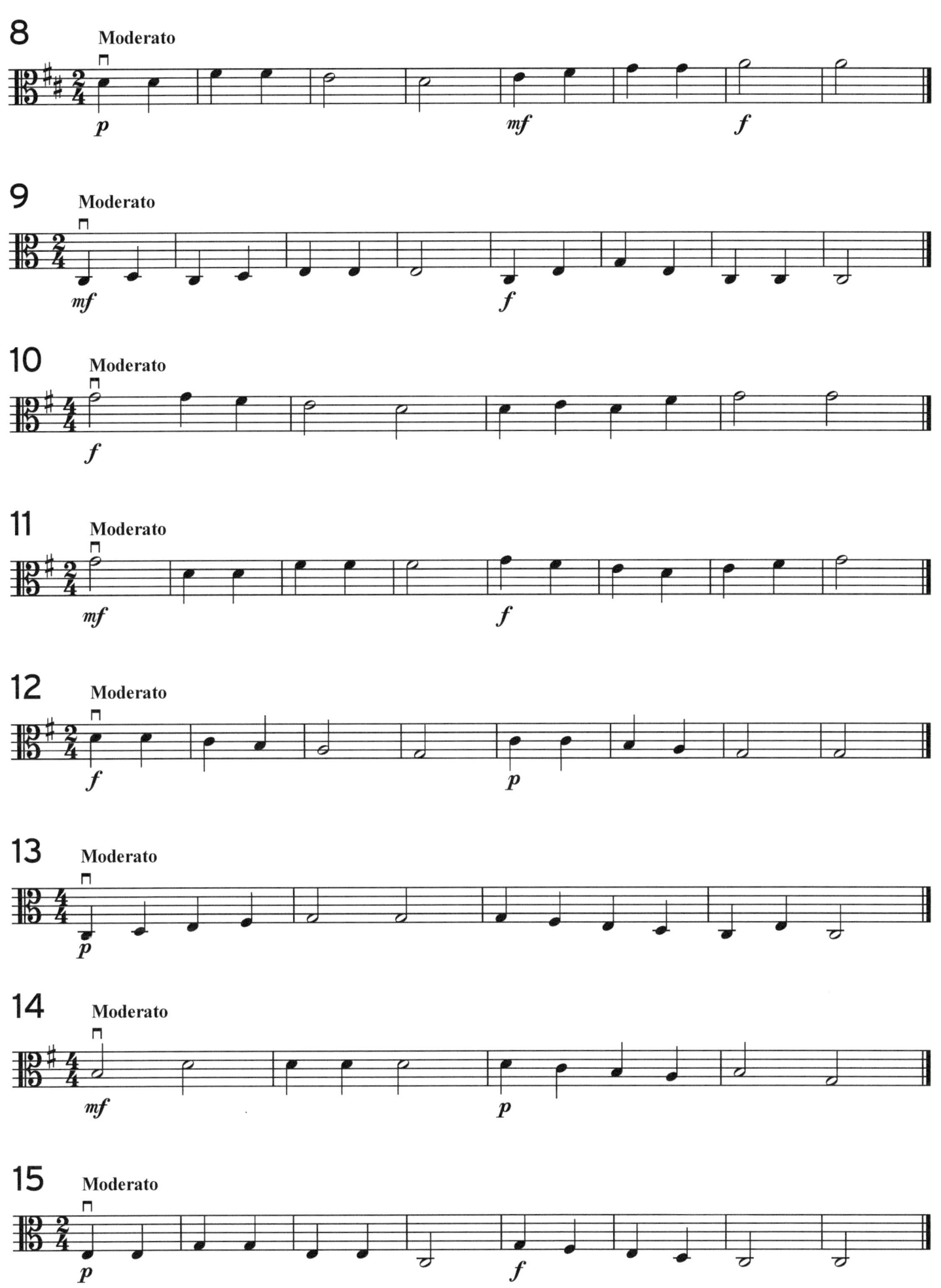

[Blank page to facilitate page turns]

Grade 2

Lesson 1

- **Practise reading the time signature 3/4 and understand the dotted minim note value**

3/4 three crotchet beats in a bar.

𝅗𝅥. **dotted minim.** A dotted minim lasts for three crotchet beats.

Play each exercise first as a rhythm on the appropriate open strings. Then play the whole exercise as written.

1

2

3

4

5

Grade 2

Think before you play:

How many crotchet beats are there in each bar?   Three ☐   Four ☐

Circle the bars that you should play on the A string.

Which finger should you use in bar 3?   2 ☐   3 ☐

How many bars in your part have more than one pitch?   One ☐   Four ☐

Duet — Set the pulse: think three crotchets and breathe in on the last one before you play.

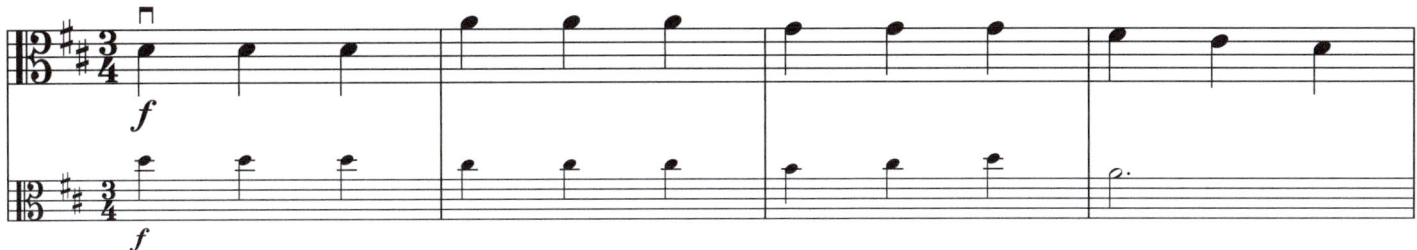

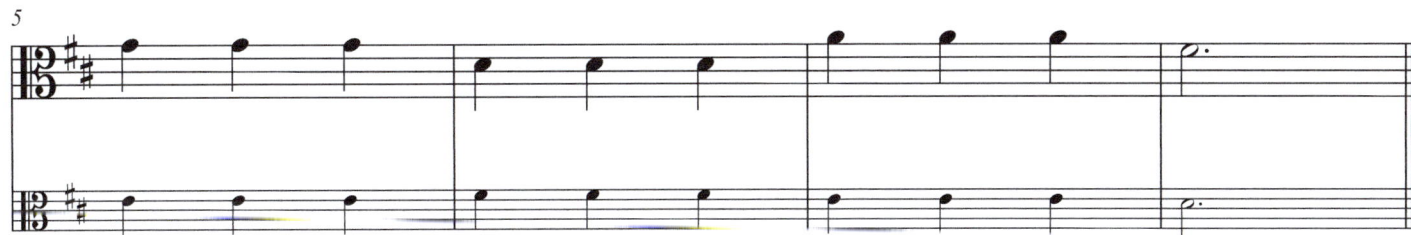

Spot check your note reading by saying the note names as you play them.

Grade 2

Lesson 2

- Practise reading semibreves and semibreve rests
- Revise the meaning of *Allegretto*

𝗈 **semibreve**. A semibreve lasts for four crotchet beats.

A semibreve rest lasts for four crotchet beats.
(The same symbol also means a whole bar of silence in any time signature.)

Allegretto means play quite fast.

Play each exercise first as a rhythm on the appropriate open strings. Then play the whole exercise as written.

1

2

3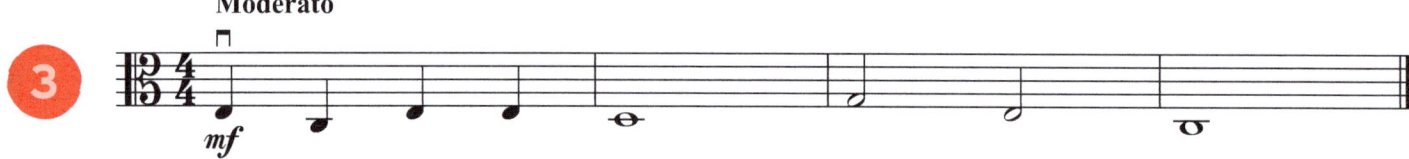

4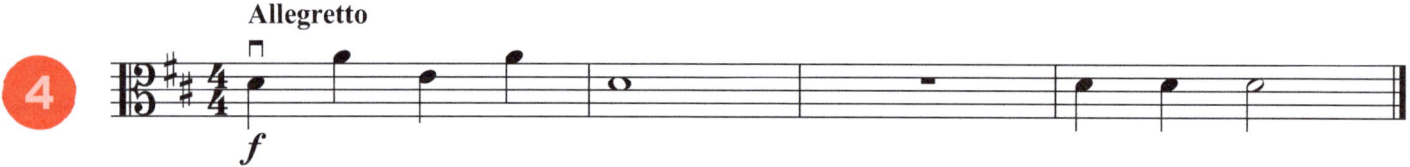

5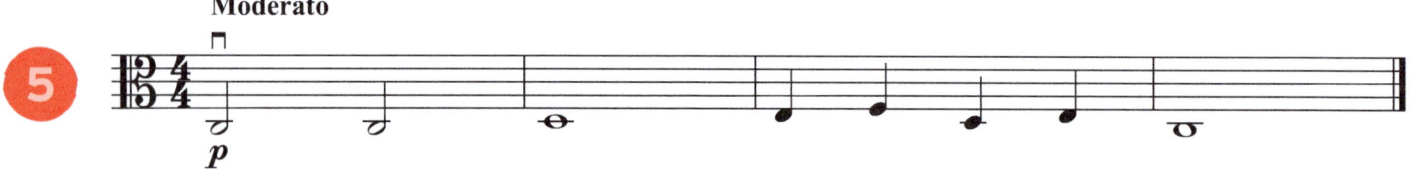

Grade 2

Think before you play:

How many crotchet beats should you count in each rest?	Two ☐	Four ☐
On which strings should you play?	G and D ☐	G and C ☐
In which bar should you change strings twice?	Bar 3 ☐	Bar 8 ☐
Which finger should you use to play the first note in bar 3?	1 ☐	2 ☐

 Set the pulse: think four crotchets and breathe in on the last one before you play.

Notice that the semibreve rests hang from the stave line: ▬

During rests, gently stop your bow on the string.

Grade 2

Lesson 3

- Practise reading two-note slurs of equal length on one string

Play the slurred notes in one bow. The notes should sound legato (smooth).

Play each exercise first as a rhythm on the appropriate open strings. Then play the whole exercise as written.

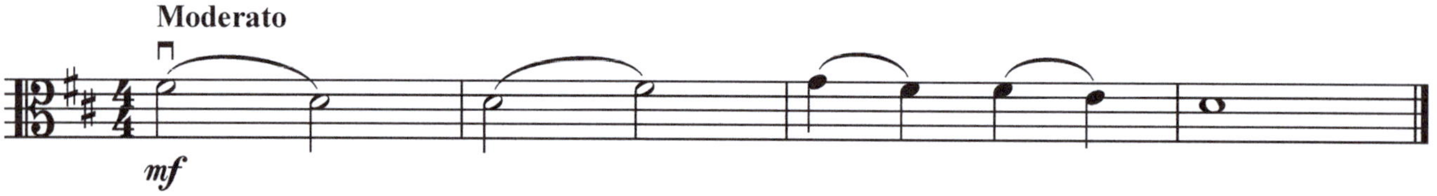

Grade 2

Think before you play:

What is the longest note value in your part?   Dotted minim ☐   Semibreve ☐

In how many bars should your **bow** play the rhythm-pattern ♩ ♩ ?   One ☐   Three ☐
(Think carefully!)

Circle the bars in which you should play only open strings.

How many bars in your part have only one pitch?   Three ☐   Five ☐

   Set the pulse: think three crotchets and breathe in on the last one before you play.

When you see a slur, remember that your bow will be moving more slowly than your left-hand fingers.

When you see:    your bow will play: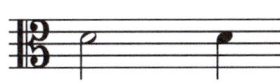

Grade 2

Lesson 4

- Practise reading two-note slurs (including two-note slurs of unequal length) on one string

Play the slurred notes in one bow. The notes should sound legato (smooth).

Play each exercise first as a rhythm on the appropriate open strings. Then play the whole exercise as written.

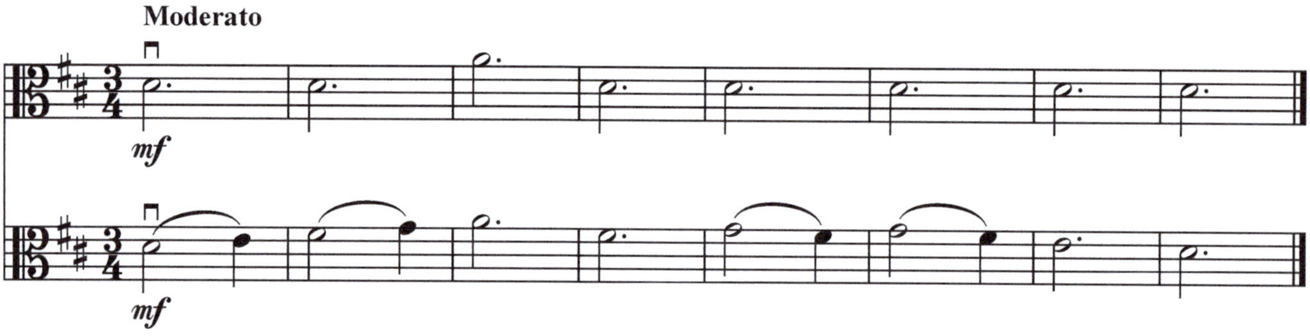

Grade 2

Think before you play:

In how many bars should your **bow** play the rhythm-pattern ♩ ♩? (Think carefully!)   Two ☐   Three ☐

Which finger should you use to play the first note of bar 3?   2 ☐   3 ☐

You should play on the C string in every bar.   True ☐   False ☐

How many bars in your part have only one pitch?   Five ☐   Six ☐

Duet   Set the pulse: think Three crotchets and breathe in on the last one before you play.

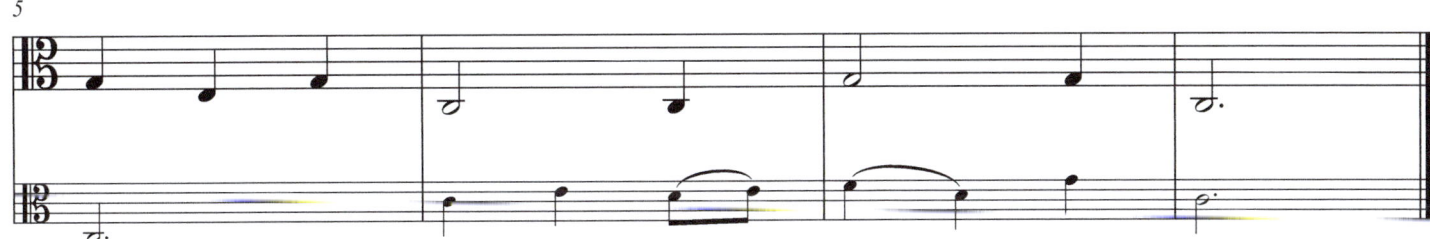

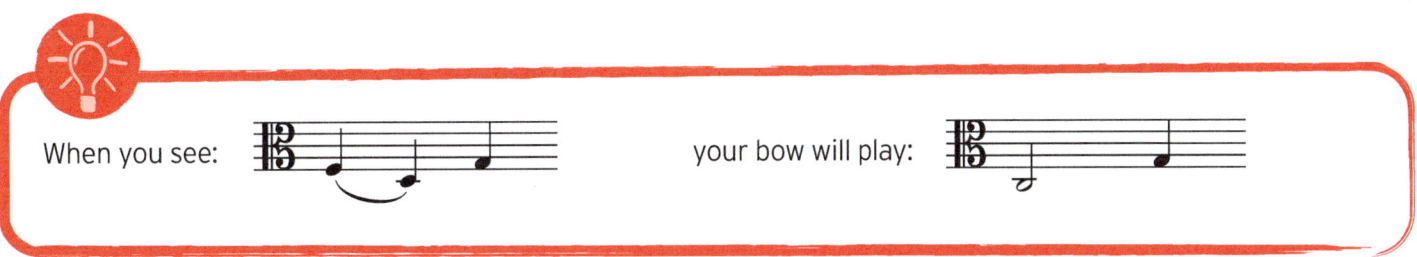

When you see: your bow will play:

Grade 2

Lesson 5

- Practise reading notes within the one-octave scale of C major

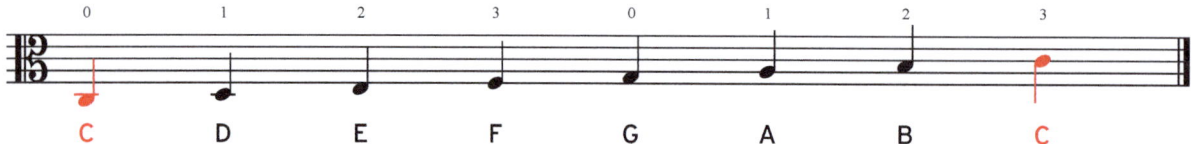

In the key of C major, the music will use notes from the C major scale.

Play each exercise first as a rhythm on the appropriate open strings. Then play the whole exercise as written.

1

2

3

4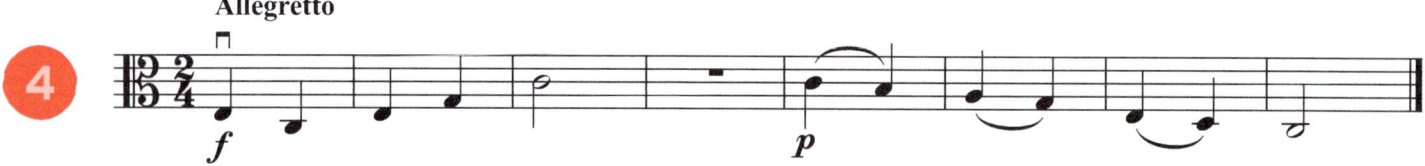

5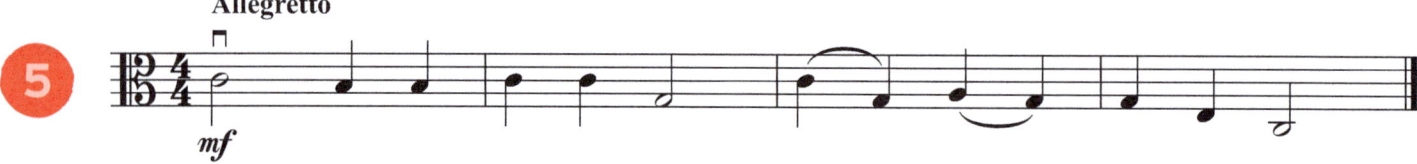

Grade 2

Think before you play:

You should play on the G string in only four bars.   True ☐   False ☐

In how many bars should you play the same rhythm as your teacher?   Three ☐   Four ☐

Circle the bars in which you can see part of C major scale (going down).

Should you play loudly or softly?   Loudly ☐   Softly ☐

 Set the pulse: think four crotchets and breathe in on the last one before you play.

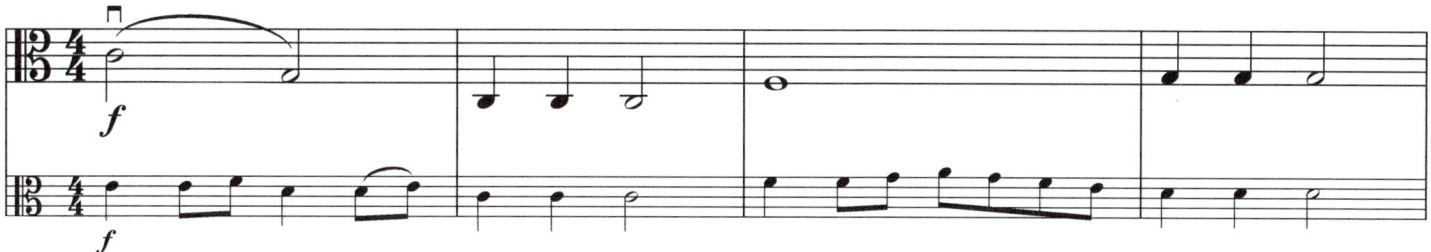

 Spotting rhythm and tune patterns will help you to become a good sight reader.

Grade 2

Lesson 6

- Practise reading notes within the one-octave scale of G major

In the key of G major, the music will use notes from the G major scale.

Play each exercise first as a rhythm on the appropriate open strings. Then play the whole exercise as written.

1 Allegretto

2 Moderato

3 Allegretto
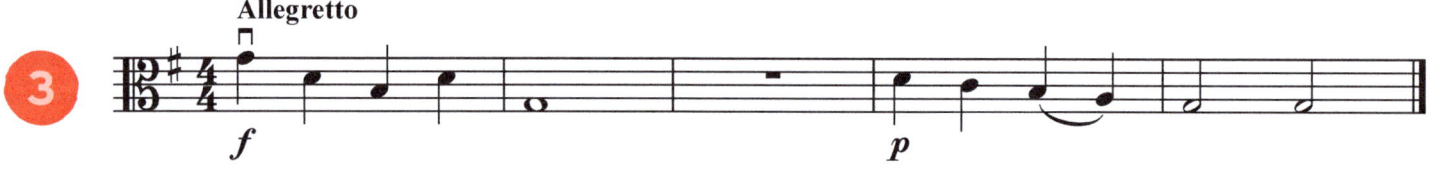

4 Moderato

5 Moderato

Grade 2

Think before you play:

From which scale should you take the notes?   G major ☐   D major ☐

What is the longest note value?   Dotted minim ☐   Semibreve ☐

Circle all the slurred notes in your part.

The dynamics stay the same throughout the piece.   True ☐   False ☐

 Set the pulse: think four crotchets and breathe in on the last one before you play.

 Whenever you play an open string, prepare your left hand for the next fingered note.

Grade 2

Lesson 7

- Practise reading notes within the one-octave scale of D major

In the key of D major, the music will use notes from the D major scale.

Play each exercise first as a rhythm on the appropriate open strings. Then play the whole exercise as written.

1

2

3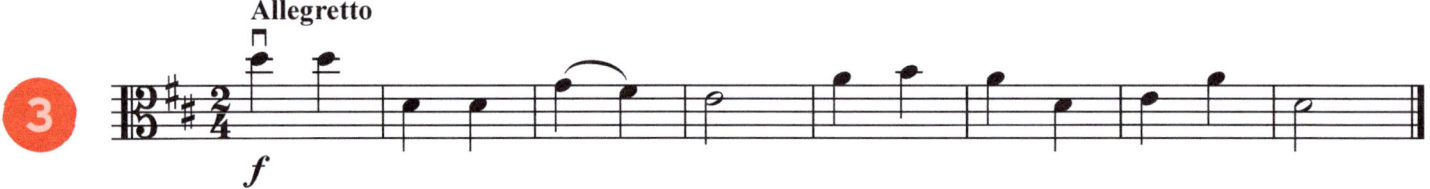

4

5

Grade 2

Think before you play:

From which scale should you take the notes?		C major ☐		D major ☐
Which finger should you use to play the first note?		2 ☐		3 ☐
Your bow should play the rhythm-pattern ♩ ♩ seven times.		True ☐		False ☐
Which is the softest bar in your part?		The first bar ☐		The last bar ☐

Duet — Set the pulse: think three crotchets and breathe in on the last one before you play.

Use your bow wisely. When playing repeats of the rhythm-pattern ♩ ♩ move your bow faster on the crotchets otherwise you will run out of bow.

Grade 2

Lesson 8

- **Practise reading tied notes**

A tie adds same-pitch note values together to make a longer note.

This D lasts for six crotchet beats: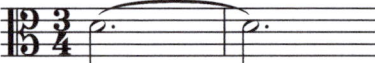

This G lasts for three crotchet beats: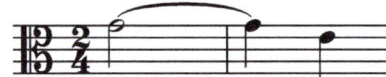

Don't repeat the tied note – your bow should keep going in the same direction.

Circle the tied notes, then play each exercise on the appropriate open strings.
Finally play the whole exercise as written.

1

2

3

4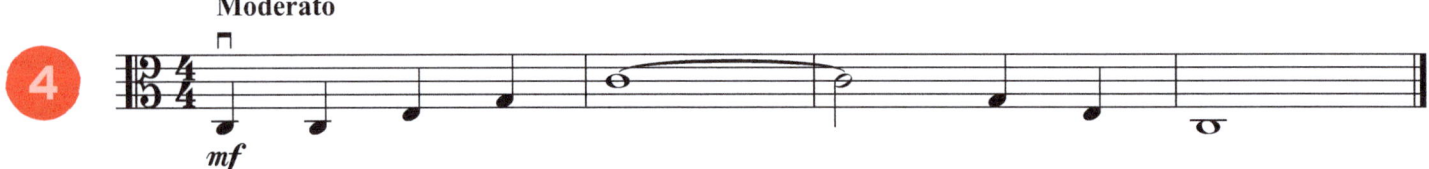

5

Grade 2

Think before you play:

On which string should you play the first tied notes? G string ☐ D string ☐

Which finger should you use to play the last note? 1 ☐ 3 ☐

You should play your part softly. True ☐ False ☐

How many 2-beat notes are there in your part? (Include tied notes.) Four ☐ Five ☐

 Set the pulse: think two crotchets and breathe in on the last one before you play.

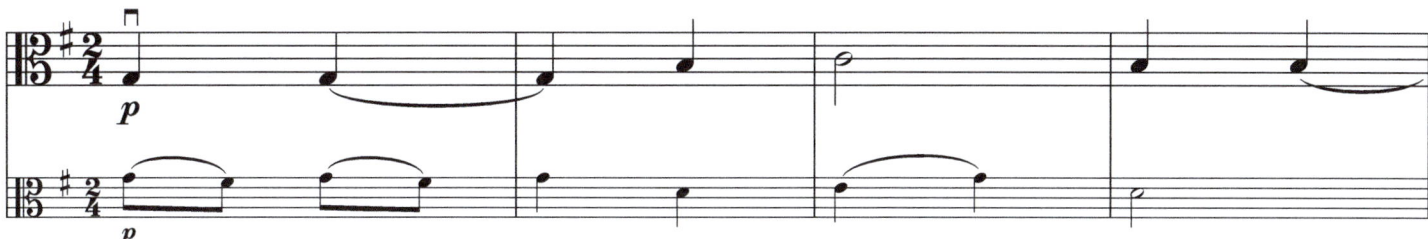

Ties add same-pitch notes together: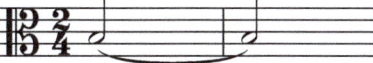

Slurs join different-pitch notes in one bow: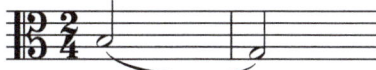

Whether you are playing ties or slurs, keep your bow moving in the same direction.

Grade 2

Lesson 9

- **Practise reading further notes in the keys of C, G and D major using standard finger patterns on the C, G and D strings**

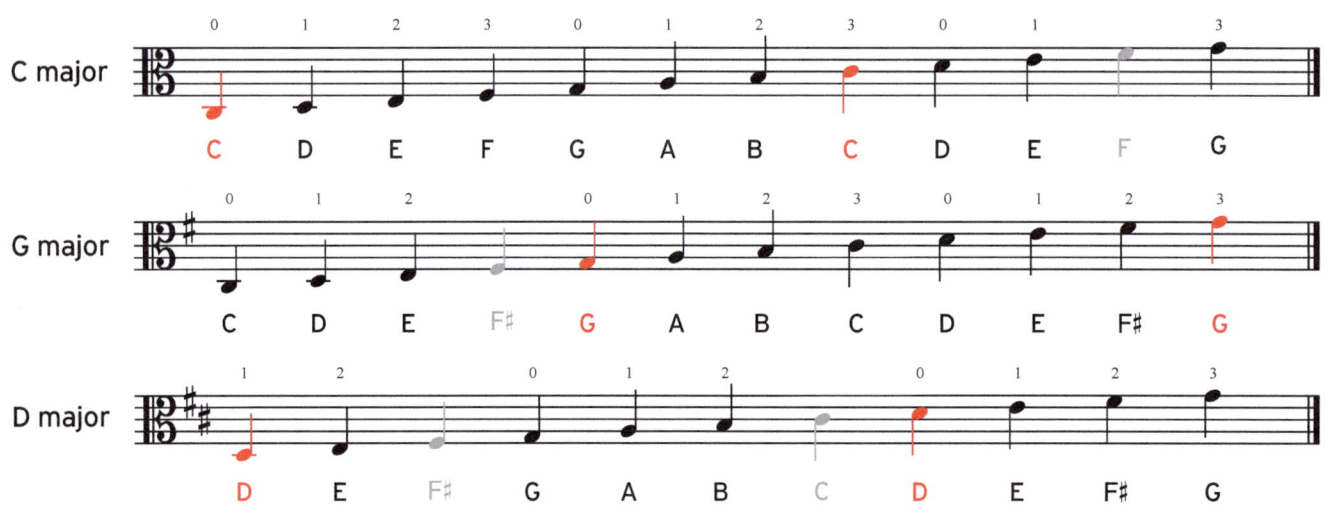

Play each exercise as a rhythm on the appropriate open strings. Then play the whole exercise as written.

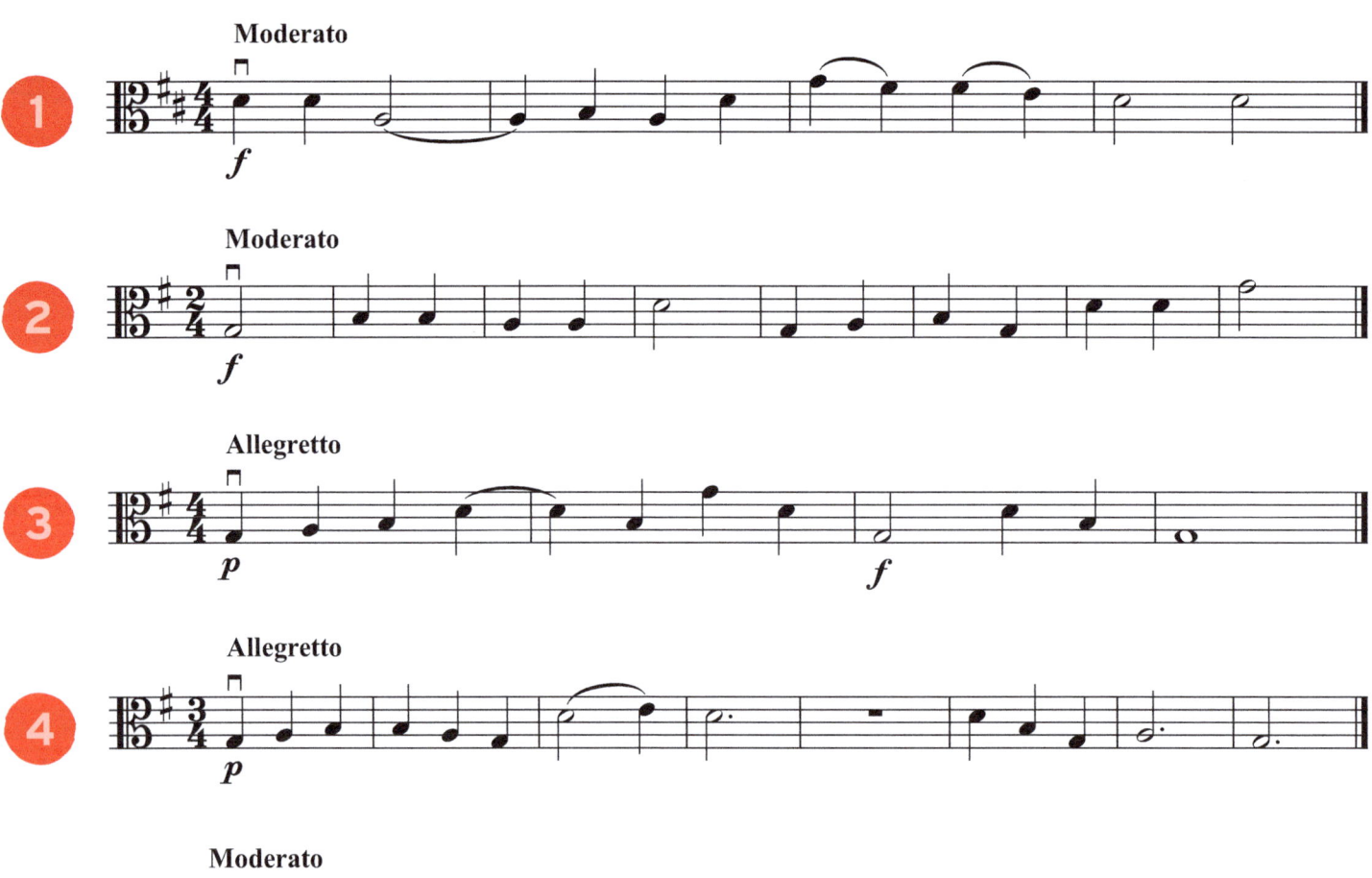

Grade 2

Think before you play:

From which scale should you take the notes? C major ☐   G major ☐

Circle the notes you should play on the C string.

Your part has a different rhythm to your teacher's part throughout. True ☐   False ☐

How many bars in your part have only minims? Two ☐   Three ☐

Duet — Set the pulse: think four crotchets and breathe in on the last one before you play.

Think about the way you use your bow. When there is a long note followed by a shorter note, you will often need to move your bow faster and more lightly on the shorter note.

Lesson 10

- Practise reading further notes in the keys of G and D major using standard finger patterns on the G, D and A strings

G major

D major

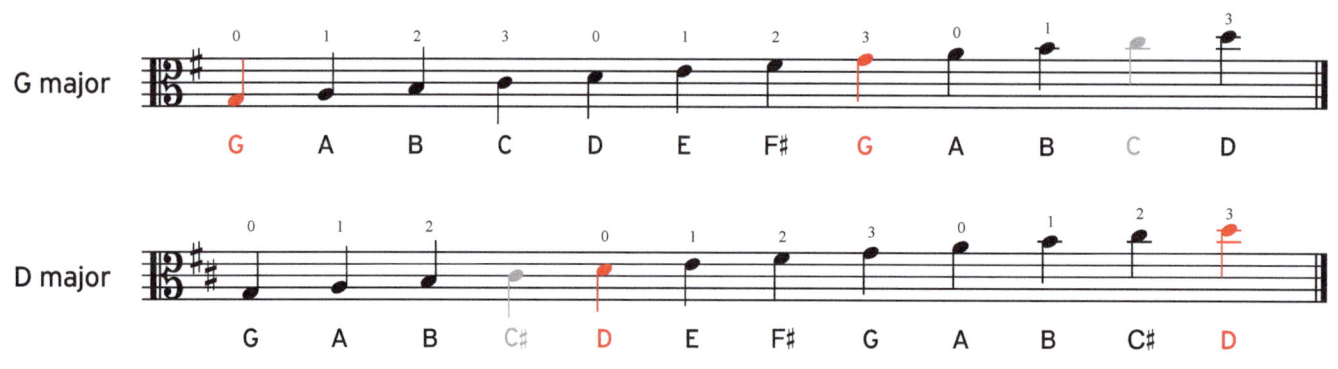

Play each exercise as a rhythm on the appropriate open strings. Then play the whole exercise as written.

1

2

3

4

5

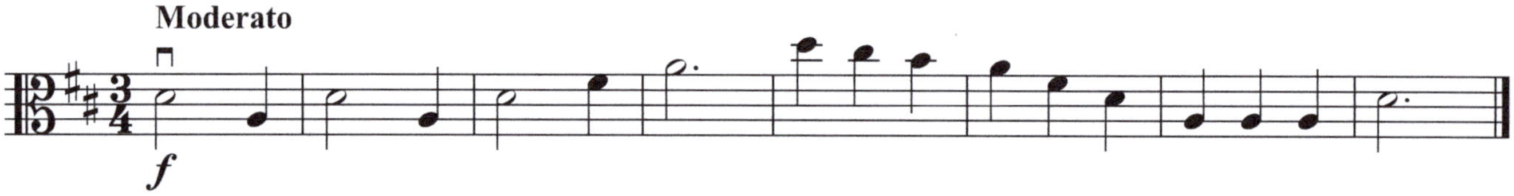

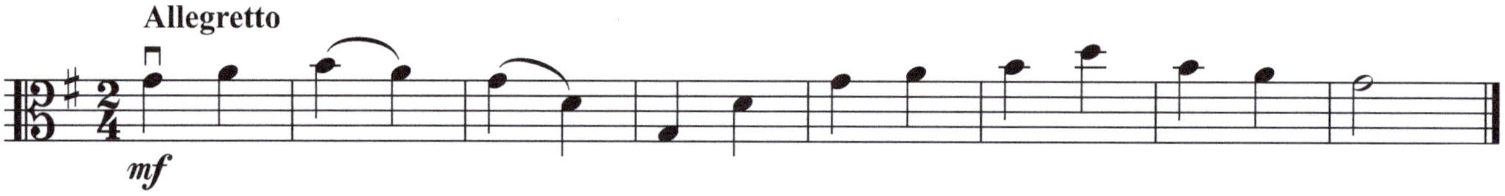

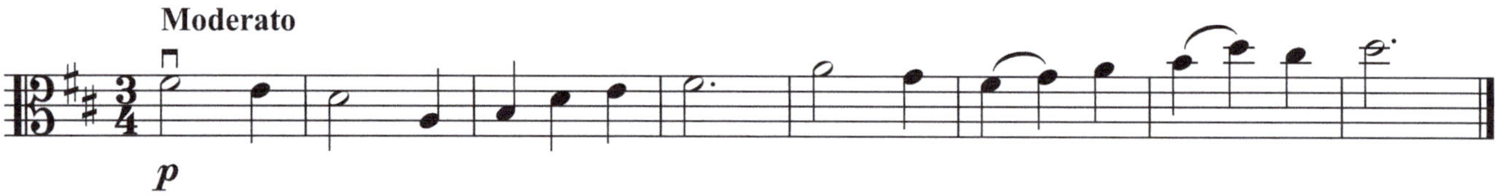

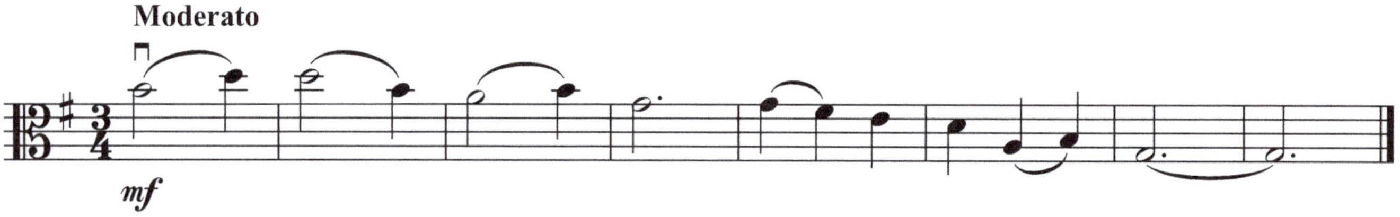

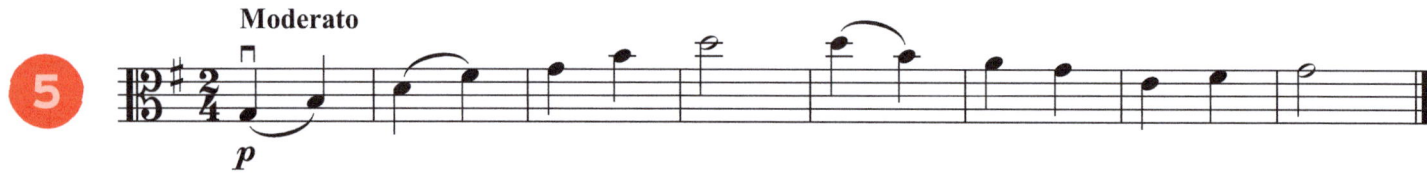

Grade 2

Think before you play:

From which scale should you take the notes?   G major ☐   D major ☐

Circle the notes you should play on the A string.

Your bow should play the rhythm-pattern ♩ ♩ ♩ six times.   True ☐   False ☐

At what tempo should you play?   Quite fast ☐   At a moderate pace ☐

Duet — Set the pulse: think four crotchets and breathe in on the last one before you play.

In Grade 2 sight reading, you may need to change strings quite often. Look ahead so that you are ready in time. When you are playing an open string, prepare your left-hand fingers so that they are ready to play the next fingered note.

Grade 2

Specimen sight reading tests

Remember to use the ideas and techniques from the previous lessons when sight reading these tests.

Grade 2

16

Allegretto

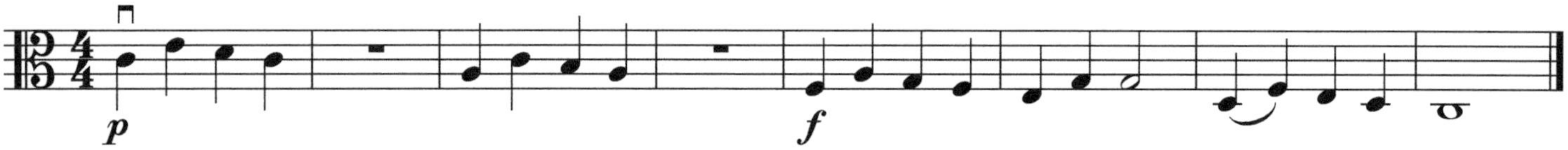

17

Moderato

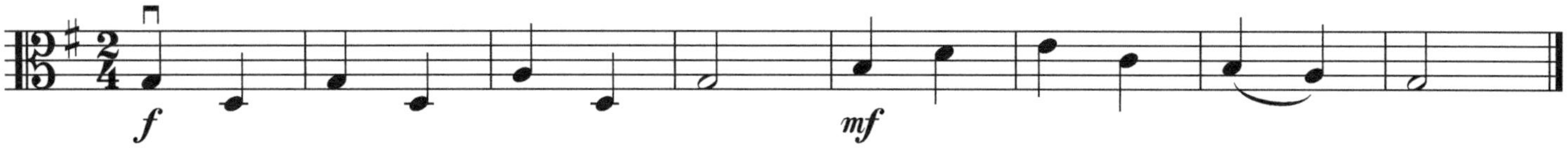

18

Moderato

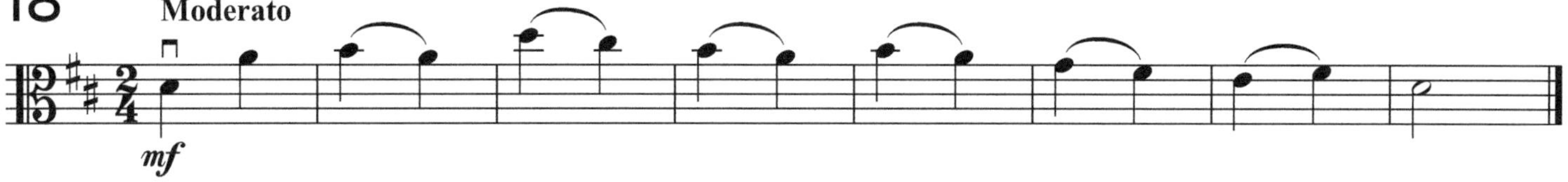

19

Allegretto

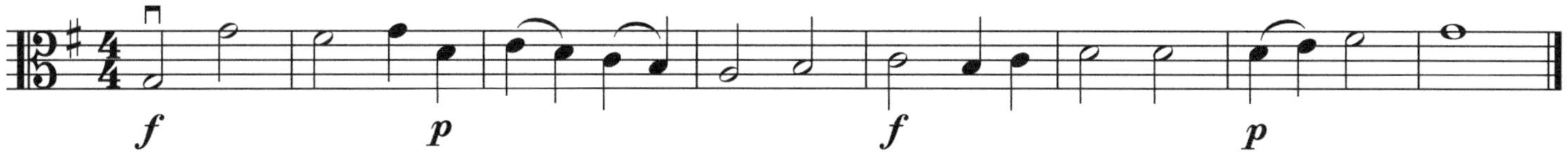

20

Allegretto

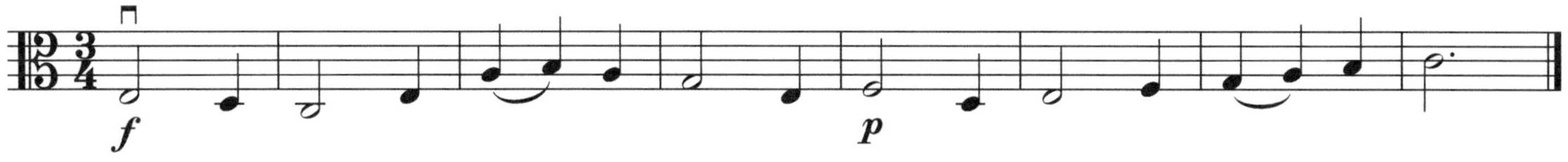

21

Moderato

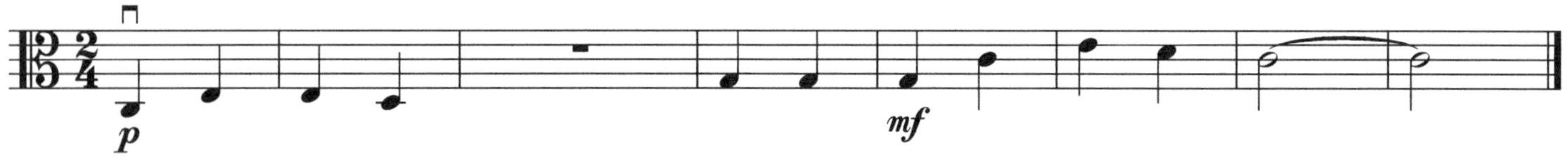

22

Allegretto

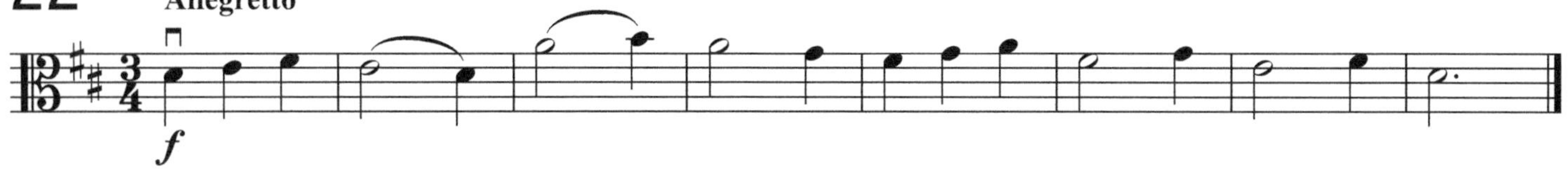